paper wings

april green

Copyright © 2016 April Green

All rights reserved. No part of this book may be reproduced in any written, electronic, recording, or photocopying without written permission of the publisher or author.

Cover Design © 2016 Mitch Green
(mgreen_green@aol.com)

Interior Design, Photography and Artwork © 2016 April Green (loveaprilgreen@outlook.com)

Model: Sasha Ray

ISBN–10:1535310812
ISBN–13:978–1535310819

i am complex and
fragile with torn paper wings.
... but i can still fly.

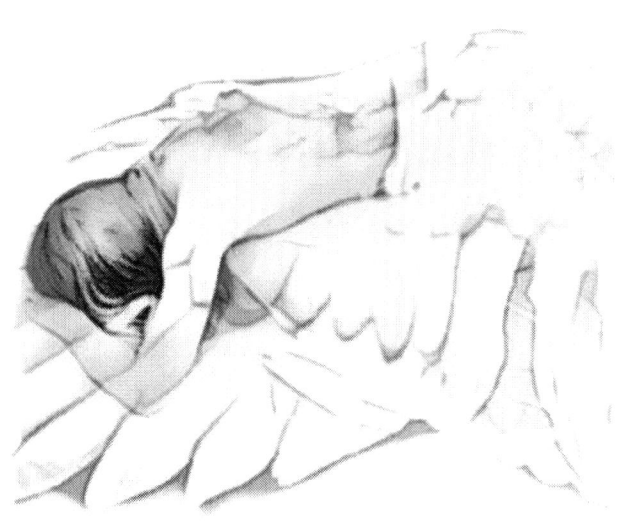

for my daughter

i am the moon
carrying the sea
in her arms.
you are my earth.
the warmth beneath
these aching bones.

a note from the author

i write to bring all that has died in me back to life.

i write because there is a hunger in my bones, which for years and years, i looked to feed using people and things outside of my being. and i broke myself hundreds of times in the process.

and now, i understand that the hunger was actually my soul; calling me home. aching for creativity. for peacefulness and mindfulness. which, in turn, brings immense happiness and fulfillment.

i write micro poetry because i like simple structure. most of my pieces are short and fragmented. broken and clipped – like wings.

i write uncapitalised, in the form of haikus, alexandrines, six words and ten words, (three lines). all of these forms cannot be titled because a title will break the structure. and if i do title my work – the titles are above or below the poem; depending on the message i wish to get across.

i like my poems to be both tender and raw – much like life.

i write about everything i have ever been —
broken. different. depressed. anxious. addicted.
orphaned. a lover. a breast cancer survivor. a
healer.

but mostly, i write in the hope that you will relate
to something, and heal whatever pain you are
holding onto.

i want you to know that, no matter how bad
things seem, something will always carry you.

— the way the moon carries the sea in her arms

april green

i wrote you some words.
i found them in the darkness,
carved into my bones.

paper wings

a body filled
with
black clouds
but
no rain
to break
them.

a p r i l g r e e n

holding the darkness
in my hands,
i try to find the light.

even just
the faint silver breath
of a dying star.

paper wings

so lost in thought...at
times – i never know if i will
find my way back.

nothing touches
the light.
a slow breathing
in the dark.
an ache i can't find.
the moon behind me…
always.
behind me.

paper wings

i have drowned
in my own sadness
many times.
it is the only place
i know where to
breathe.

april green

words that weep in your
mouth
before you even speak.

come to me exactly as you are.
because i am here.
in front of you.
and i do not see your scars.

— the kind of words i want to hear

april green

flesh.
embroidered
in violets
and black
tears.
climbing
vines
wrapped in
paper white
skin.

— dying for the light

— the other side of silence

tell me about
the other side of silence.
for i have this inexplicable hunger
for something my hands can't reach
but my soul longs for.
and it is not of this world.
but i have known it.
i have felt it;
stepping over my ribs
like a flightless bird.
it is a hunger for something
that never comes.

— desire

desire that splits you at the seams.
ribbons tangled around broken bones;
pulled apart with longing.

paper wings

i wish i could unhide
the hidden within me.

ghosts.
embodied in all the things
i have ever looked upon
with love.
as though i am from
another world.
as though i do not
belong here.

paper wings

every day, i dive deeper
and deeper into the sea of shame.
wave after wave
mounting like wings of steel.
until my bones break in two.
until my body turns to salt.
and still i drown.
still i drown.

april green

— raw

days when i feel
too over–exposed.
the way a blade of sunlight
can suddenly cut through the neck
of a sheltered rose.

paper wings

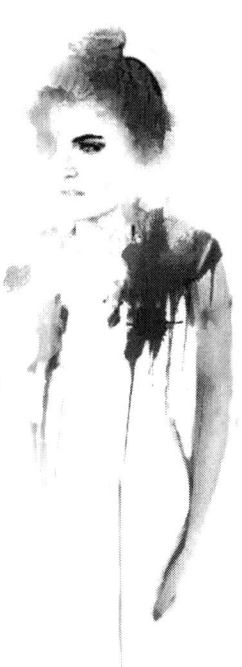

— humans

you try to make me
feel whole and break me
at the same time.
so while you look
into my eyes – i have
already disappeared.

april green

here you are,
wanting to enter my world
but not strong enough to
carry it.

paper wings

i am tired of talking.
please can we speak
in silence
like we did when we were
stars?

april green

— crushed whispers

you leave words
in my hands and then
walk away.

paper wings

i vanish inside my own silence.

april green

all of this broken time...
all of these feathers
and wings
and bones.
scarred with memory.
like little fossil footprints.

– running from the past

paper wings

pain so deep
you dare not speak about it
for fear of disturbing it.

april green

the kind of remembering
that holds you in the air.
holds your breath in its hands
until you're forced to feel it.

— the kind that stops time

sometimes,
there is more pain in a memory
than in the moment
itself.

april green

my body is torn with
the shame of what it is
doing to itself.
my hands burn
all the time.

paper wings

i pull myself apart
and sew myself back
together again.
every day.

this i know –

my soul does not
belong
in the skin i feel
most comfortable in.
because the skin
i feel most comfortable in
is numb.
yet, my soul...
it is like a burning
sun.

(sometimes my hunger both cages me in and
drives me out of my skin)

paper wings

memory traces
itself
into the carbon
of my bones.
trembling
before i even
remember.

the kind of self–inflicted
suffering
that stays with you.
like ink onto bones.
indelible bruises under
the skin.

paper wings

— untie me

help me disentangle
my mind from yours.
for it is wrapped too tight
and i fear i will lose
myself.

april green

some days, my stone white heart
crumbles like the falling moon.

paper wings

when the past
seeps out in front of you
and you can do nothing
but live with it
one more time.

a p r i l g r e e n

the words i write have
a memory of their own.

— i am just the ink

paper wings

you keep pulling
at the strings of my heart;
unaware it has already
come undone.

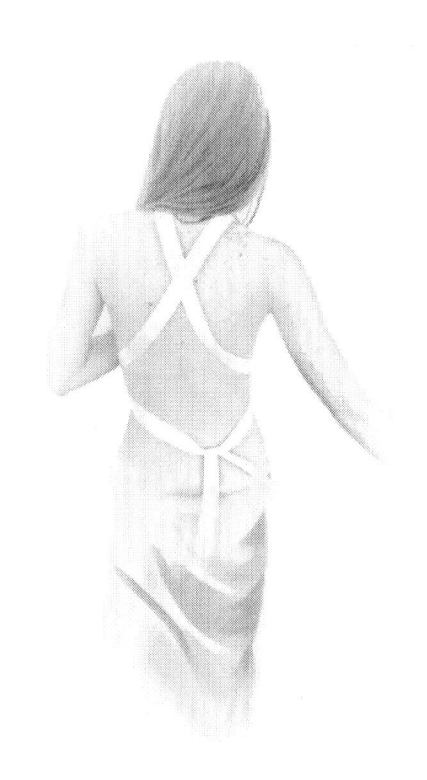

april green

i have always felt something
above me; like a breath before
i breathe.
and i am never quite sure
who is looking out of my
eyes.

— sometimes, i can hear silence listening

paper wings

prayers.
aching
and sighing
and falling from my mouth
like hidden answers.
as though something
deep within
was begging
them to
appear.

april green

— revelation

the thing that keeps
breaking me,
cannot possibly
fix me.

— revelation ii

when i fill the hole from within,
i breathe gold.
when i fill the hole from without,
it gets deeper
and
emptier
and
hungrier
for more.

april green

it fills my heart
how well the broken
understand me.

paper wings

some memories never
leave your bones. like
salt in the sea; they become
part of you.

– and you carry them

april green

paper wings

and now…
i must leave you.
for if i do not leave you,
i will leave myself.

a p r i l g r e e n

a little piece of moonlight
has settled inside my
bones.

paper wings

a whisper of night falls from the stars
into my hands.
abandoned dreams returning from the sky.

— and i hold them

april green

i know this feeling.
the look in my eyes.
the distance.
the silence.
the gold dust
of the soul
etching
words onto bone.

— it is the transformation
of me into me
again

paper wings

and i heard her say:
"darling,
remember your roots.
you are like a wild flower.
you must grow…

but you must also
let go."

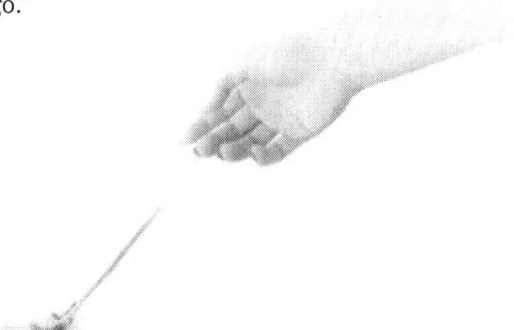

april green

and my delicate bones
whispered the soft language
of hope...

paper wings

in the darkness
my body is a garden.
closed buds of silence
spilling seeds of dreams.

april green

skin
like a veil.
lifting to the silent
world within.
to the language
of stars.

paper wings

— the broken

there is a pureness
emanating from the broken.
a beauty encasing them.
like porcelain air.
a halo within a tear.
and it is not because
they learned how to put themselves
back together again.
no.
it is because they met
their souls in the process.

a tender touch of rain
in the stillness of your
bones.
an indigo sky
breaking behind
your spine.

– i am the silent storm
you didn't know was
coming

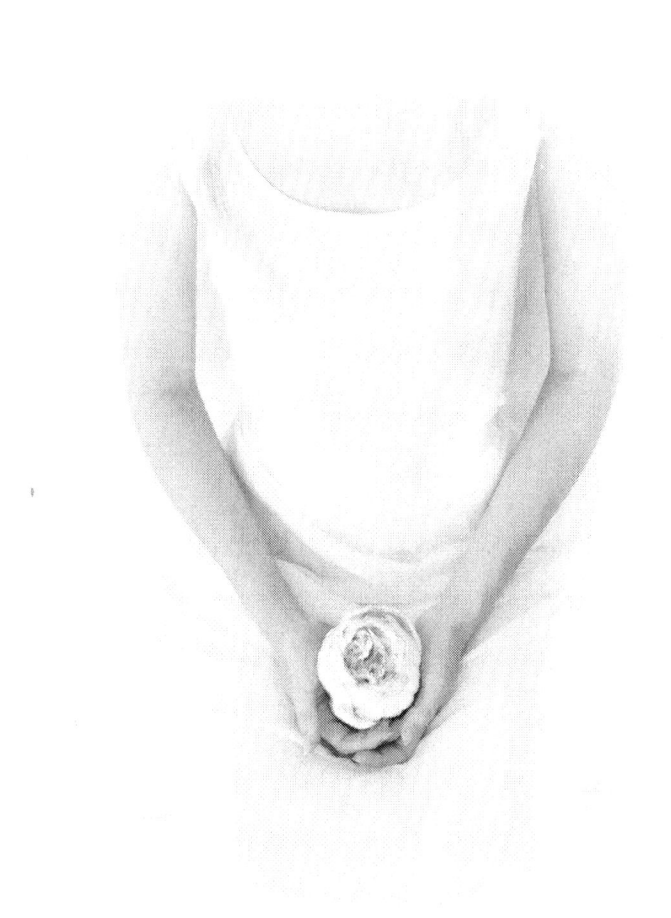

april green

— summer rain

invisible ink
blotting paper
white skin.
torn shadows
falling like ash.
and with the glowing
embers
i write.

i am writing.

i am writing
my bones clean.
i am untying the scars
from my flesh
and starting
again.

— silent language

when you meet
a certain person...
it's the soul that knows.
it's the soul that
remembers.
hearts within a heart.
bones from the same
clay.

april green

it was a memory
i felt when i met
you.

the kind of memory
that breaks open ancient
stars.

paper wings

you are the light my
soul walks towards...you are the
dawn i remember.

april green

give me a minute...
the moon is dressing my bones
in white silk for you.

paper wings

she is delicate.
like a fragment of sunshine.
like a falling leaf.

april green

and she sits on the
edge of solitude and waits
for the moon to speak.

p a p e r   w i n g s

she ties ribbons around broken bones.

april green

sometimes,
she wanders
into another world.
naively.
like a lost child.

and when
she comes back,
she always has
the stars in her eyes.
the moon on her lips.

april green

minds we can never
see inside of…just feel.
like little earthquakes.
like magic.
a wave within a wave.

paper wings

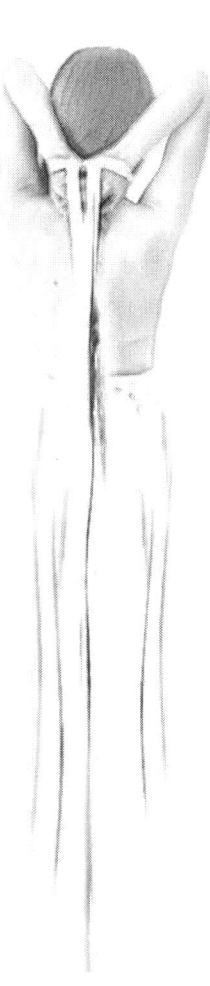

— you

the allure of you.
the soft ache between
my spine.
the scent of promise
unfolding
beneath your bones.
you.
i can't escape
you.

april green

you are a storm
about to break in my
heart.

paper wings

you are something like me.
will you stay until morning then
fold me back into the fallen
moon?

april green

asleep in the silk
silence; bodies wrapped around
the echo of love.

paper wings

whatever she does,
it is always so beautiful.
the poetry.
the silence.
the pain.

– it is always so beautiful

april green

i like the way you look at me.
as though you're memorising me
so you never forget.

paper wings

come into my dreams tonight...
and bring me a piece of the moon.

april green

and even if i tried to love you
more;
i am certain the sky would fall
into the sea.

paper wings

— how do you do this?

you touch my darkness
with the most beautiful
kind of light.
you hold me as though
i'm a burning star,
just fallen into your arms.
as though i'm something
you remember from centuries
ago.

— home

i want to get closer than your skin.
to unfasten the silver lining and climb inside.
i want to open your moon white ribs
and dissolve into every piece of you.
until there is no distance between us.
until we are melted down to stars.
until we are home.

paper wings

nights when we poured the sunset over our bones
and came back to life.

nights when we made sleep wait behind the door.
as though it would stop time.

april green

and my love for you
deepens...like the colour of
rain upon the sea.

paper wings

the closer you are
to me
the less words i need.
it's that place
in our souls
where there is
no language for.

– love me there

april green

paper wings

all the pain within
me softly burns away when
you are next to me...

april green

— teach me

teach me how to love myself
the same way you love me.
show me to myself.
i want to see what you see.

paper wings

poetry.
resting in the lush
of your mouth
like burning gold.

speak to me.

i will crumble to ash
in your hands.

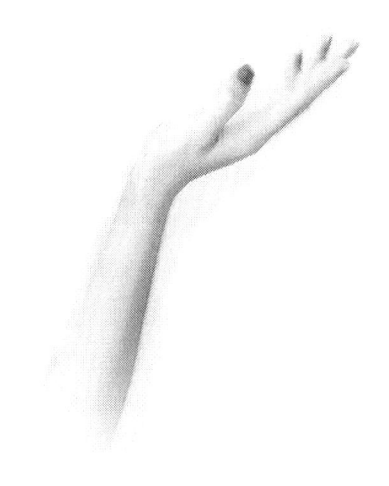

april green

some people can leave
you lost for words in the most
beautiful kind of way.

paper wings

– hold me

hold me in this love.
for when you go away,
i become exhausted
with the drowning.
with the salt of my tears.

april green

– lost in flowers

and our love is lost.
in flowers. in the breeze.
in the trembling tide
that steals you away from me.
in all the beauty.
all the pain.
all the poetry we carve
into the air.

our love is lost.

april green

the kind of hurt
that teaches
a kind of tender.

paper wings

and i cling to you;
the way rain clings to a black sky.
like a tapestry of silver thread.
pinning down the moon.

and still... you break free
by morning.

april green

the way they leave you
and stay
at the same time.

paper wings

still.
i am happy with the thought of you.
that is enough.

– alchemy

a love so intense
even the flames will die
with us.
and then.
we will love in dust.

i will wait for this love.
i will wait for you.

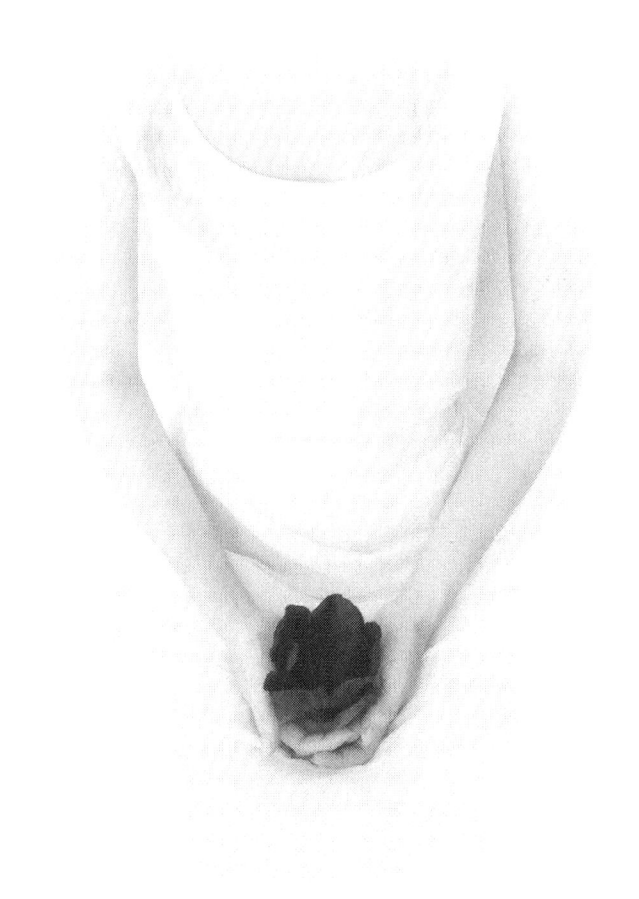

april green

death stitches
the taste of loss
inside my mouth
and i dare not
speak.

like tremors
erupting in a body of water.
steel waves breaking speech.
fractured words
falling from flesh; like rotting leaves.
scalding tears.
like burning ink on paper thin skin.
black ache.
thunder bruising cloud.
tender.
like someone else's skin.
lead bones treading air.
moon pulling down sky.
drowning but never dying.

— grief

april green

a mind filled with your silence.

paper wings

— without you

i listen to the soft weeping
of my heart, like the ocean
in darkness.
tears of the tide
washing over the face of the earth.
the salt of lost souls.

and i cry for them.

i cry for us.

in my dreams,
i watch you parting
the sea of grief.

in my dreams,
i feel you unstitching
the seam of the earth
and holding me
once more.

paper wings

the taste of rain
on my skin
and memory
in my throat.
softly swelling.
like a path
of wild flowers.

april green

fragments of you
the light left behind.
fingerprints pressed
into air.

— the weight of stardust upon earth

paper wings

in my forbidden dreams,
the whispering wind
carries me to you.
and in these dreams –
i am awake more than
ever before.

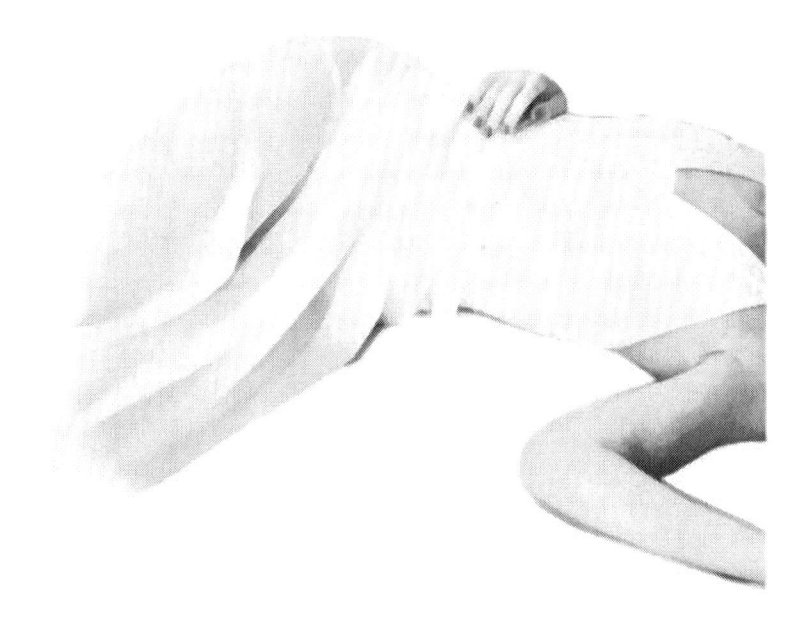

april green

i cannot remove
the thought of you.
it has stained my soul
like a watermark.
it is tangled around
your absence
like a haunted sigh.
like an invisible shape,
shifting through memories,
pressing them onto bone.
and i wake to your voice
in my hands.
my heart on the floor.

paper wings

even on the darkest of days;
you are a shadow that never
leaves my side.
a tender reminder,
resting beneath my skin.
like the echo of an ancient
heartbeat.
it is as though you are the sun.
rising in my bones.
reminding me to keep
breathing.

a p r i l   g r e e n

hide the moon from me tonight.

paper wings

it is in my head that
i find you most often.
sometimes, more often
there,
than you ever were
here.

— you are summer

sleeping under my
ribs.
an injured bird
beneath a tree.
and still; you sing under
the weight of a dying
spring.

— and now you are sky

reflecting onto the skin
of the sea.
like ribbons of light;
woven between hands.
like dripping honey;
embedded into flesh.
a body of gold.
treading water.
breaking together.
softly.
like the salt in my tears.
the sand in my bones.

and i dissolve
into every piece of you
once more.

april green

the way loss quietly
curls around ribs.
like hands;
tugging at the most
tender
piece of the heart.

paper wings

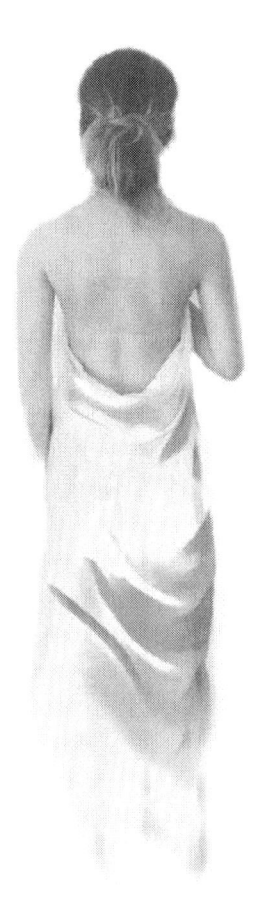

nights when i wear
nothing
but the ghost of you.

april green

your absence is
splitting the moon in half
every night.

— come back to me

i will give you every fragment
of my light; if only you would
come back to me.

i want you to know that when you hand me
the moon every night – i always read the letter
that you tuck inside her spine.

paper wings

i can still taste you;
the midnight blue quartz
of your bones.
the sweet white flowers
in your voice.
pressing against me
like a memory.
like a delicate scent.

and like a pearl on a chain;
i tremble under the weight
of your absence.

a p r i l g r e e n

and then i go to
that place in my mind where i
can see you once more.

paper wings

you are the ache
that sits in my empty
hands.

april green

you are a scent
upon my skin.
a memory;
captured in a
certain light.
like dust.
you are a poem,
etched like raw silver
into the lining
of my heart.
a silken stream
of thought,
braided between ribs.
never to be untied
from my being.

paper wings

nights when my spine folds
into a half dark moon;
and all i want to do
is explode into a million black stars
to be with you once more.

april green

i am loving you silently.
i am trying to live within the space
you left behind.

paper wings

tonight...
i will unfold the sky
and worship you
upon
the altar of moonlight.

and i will hold you.

— the eternal dust between my palms

a p r i l g r e e n

beautifully tragic
is the broken heart
that still beats
under the weight
of its keeper's
sorrow...

paper wings

in all the still and silent
space.
between thinking.
between breathing.

— there you are

april green

i break open the moon
and find fragments of you.

— petrichor

do you remember
the night when it rained
and you said it belonged to us?
that was the night i loved you
the most.

send me some of your rain.
wherever you are.
even if it falls when i'm
asleep.

i want to wake to you
once more.

april green

i still hold onto you;
from a distance.
the way starlight holds onto
the vast void of night.

— the way we hold onto darkness

paper wings

— ash

i write all that you left behind.
empty paper bones.
lined in carbon.
pressing words left unsaid.

even after all this time,
i still feel closest to you
in the arms of midnight.
when the moon is full of longing
and the stars fall with each breath.
because i know you are awake too.
and in the low, aching light –
i am certain i can hear you
praying for me.

early.
while the grief
is still asleep.
and the
remembering
hasn't curled around
my throat
like hands.
i try to let
the prayer
hold me.

april green

and when you taste the
rain, do you feel me closer
than ever before?

paper wings

i sleep inside your dreams.
that haunting ache
pressing against you.
tender.

— like the moon against the sky

when i think about you –
i reach out to touch you.
but you are not here...
then i feel you;
moving under my opaline skin.
embracing my broken bones.
putting me back together.
and i realise...
you're still here.
like the moon in the daylight sky.

– you will always be still here

– feather and bone

i have learned how to live
in two places at once.
because i can feel you;
looking into my dreams.
like rain against glass.
from a place outside of time.
a place we came from.
like the edge of eternity.
between feather and bone.
earth and sky.
moonlight balancing dust.

and in the nude light before dawn;
dissolving into the seam of the earth,
like a footprint of gold.

i walk with you once more.

april green

just one minute in
your arms and i would never
let time start again.

paper wings

i am trying to learn
from the ancient stars...
i am trying to let go
and burn even brighter
than before.

a p r i l   g r e e n

i will return to you
wrapped in moonlight
and dust.

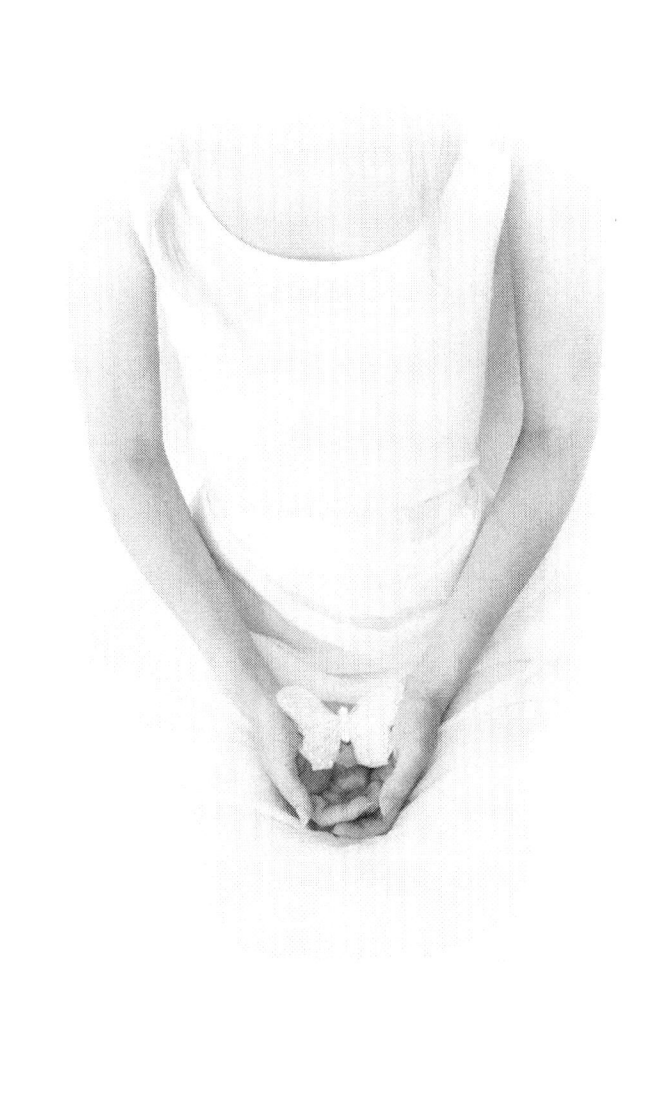

april green

i am drawn to the broken souls
who have clawed their way out of
the darkness using their own light.

— broken wings

to the self-loathers. the self-fixers who seek anesthetic in everything they touch. the ones who keep a whole language inside the lining of their skin, which flows fluent like a river in their veins and doesn't ever stop.
the ones who don't want to feel the pain but when the numbness becomes too much; want to feel it one more time in order to forget it one more time.
the ones who hate themselves for what they keep doing to themselves but keep doing it to themselves because they hate themselves.
the ones who can't see a way out because they have fallen too far in.

please believe me — there are other people out there who feel exactly the same as you do.
find them.

'i can do this on my own' is denial because the way you are harming yourself is showing you that you can't. so you have to get on your knees and tell the air that you can no longer do this alone.
you have to find the strength to fall.

that's when something will step in and carry you. that's when something will slowly put you back together.

but you have to ask. you have to ask.

because some battles can only be won
by surrendering.

april green

break open the pure,
silent tears that fall.
for they contain a message
from your soul.

paper wings

i care not for the pain
but for the lesson it will
teach me.

april green

lay down.
let the moon unstitch
the day from your skin.

paper wings

and when dawn comes;
like a luminous moment
wearing nothing but a dress
of translucent air...

open her up.

breathe her.

april green

soft
is the light
when it arrives.
like a slow wave,
breaking gently
on the shore.

– returning

some kind of humans...
wanting to know where the look
in my eyes leads to.
asking me where my thoughts have been.
trying to tame my wandering soul.

you should know this:

— you can't fold a burning star back into the sky

if i am not enough for you
then you are not enough for yourself.
you have a hole in your soul
that only you can fill.

do not depend on me
to make you feel better.
do not ask me to fill your hole.

— i am busy filling my own

paper wings

and after all this time...
i finally understand that
i will never find completeness
with another person.
how can another complete me?
how can they fill a hole that
never belonged to them
in the first place?

— hands that do not belong to me
cannot 'make' me

– skin

this skin.
like the sea;
nude and
raw and stained
with salt.
like white lace.
like crushed bones
of the tide.
of ancestors.
holding
wild flesh.
naked with truth.
remembering.
this skin.
like the skin
i wore
as a child.

i am
learning to wear
this skin
again.

– hidden

no–one can give you anything
you do not already possess.
they can just bring it out of you.
stir an emotion. pull back a layer.
but it was always there to begin with.

you thought they gave it to you didn't you?
and when they left;
you thought they took it away.

how?

when it was always yours to begin with.

you do not need
a lover
to be a lover.
you have endless love
in your heart —
enough to move the stars closer to earth.

— when will you start giving it to yourself?

paper wings

can you feel my words
still breathing when you read them?
i wrote them for you.

april green

paper wings

to remain
in my own skin.
to belong
only to myself.

— this is all i ever want

in my solitude
i want nothing but silence.

— the universe speaks

paper wings

keep breaking… for birds
will fly from your ribs once the
light starts to get through.

— the healer

the reason you are carrying pain
is to remind yourself that you are
in need of healing.
so you have to reach in.
you have to reach in to where the pain is.
to the most broken place of your being.
even if you cut yourself in the process.
you have to be brave.
burn a little.
expose yourself a little.
you will feel vulnerable.
and raw.
and naked.
all the things you never dared to be.
but this is the place where the healing sits.
it sits inside the pain.

and god, will you look beautiful
once you've walked through that
fire.

paper wings

we spend our lives
begging for answers,
when the symphony
of truth has been playing within
our hearts all along.

— dream snatchers

the voices of others.
the kind of voices that feel like weeds,
tangling around flowers.
the ones where they question you.
create doubt within you.
make you curse yourself.
feel stupid. a dreamer.
and you can feel the fire going out.
you can feel it cooling beneath your ribs;
as though someone has reached in
and blown it out with one single breath.
and later; you hear them again in your head.
and you can't tell the difference between
their voice or your voice.
so you put out the fire yourself.
you kill your own dreams.

ignore these voices.
keep your dreams between yourself
and the air you breathe before sleep.
because these are the voices of their own pain.
these are the voices of their own self–doubt.
these are the voices of an unconscious repetition
called 'fear.'

paper wings

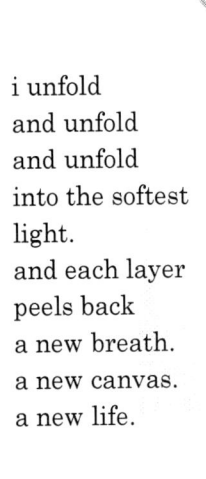

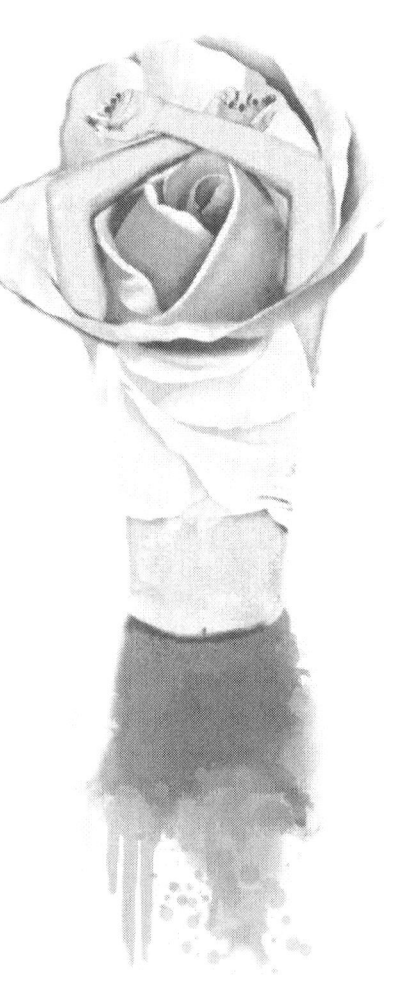

i unfold
and unfold
and unfold
into the softest
light.
and each layer
peels back
a new breath.
a new canvas.
a new life.

april green

i know who i am now.

when the sky disguises
your tears with rain —
cry hard.
for this is mother nature's
way of taking care of you.

— the softening

april green

the silence after
rain... how quickly the sky pulls
herself together.

paper wings

the steady song
in your heart.
the one that sings
at dawn
like the birds.

— listen to this song

— heart

sometimes i wonder why
i have never called a home a home.
i wonder why i have never wanted to either.
and i think it's because i have always known
that i have a home. i am a home.
i have never really belonged anywhere
because i have only ever belonged to myself.

and now.
it warms my heart
to know that wherever i go –
i take my home with me.

paper wings

come home to yourself.
your soul has tales
to sing.

april green

when you are hungry
for something.
it is usually for your own
soul.

— stay together

paper wings

if the pain
is not going away,
then you are not
listening
to what it is telling you.

april green

— becoming

all the days of hurting
will add up to something.
these are the days when the truth
is working its way out of your bones.
the days when enough
is becoming enough.
the days when *you*
are becoming.

april green

in time,
you don't suffer
any less.
you just learn that pain
is what you make of it
using your mind.
in time,
you learn
how to control
your mind.

paper wings

sometimes silence
is simply contentment.
i live in my own world.
i am happy here.

— i think it is the place
of my soul

the problem is that
we fall in love with
the future too much.

— we fall in love with illusions

paper wings

beauty is born
out of pain.
not out of perfection.

april green

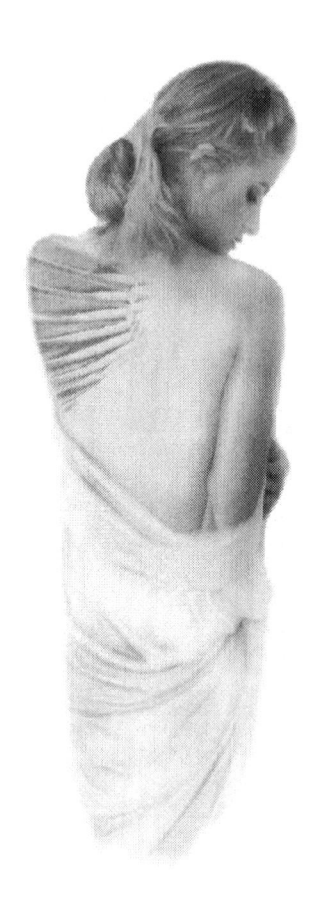

— you are standing in the answer

it is when you start to lose yourself that you start to look for yourself in other people...other things. but if the sun climbed into the moon, there would be no light.

there is a place and a time in your life that links you to the person you were before all the chaos. all the pain. all the heartache. before you looked in the mirror and judged the reflection looking back at you.

find this place. go back to this place.
because, in this place, you knew exactly who you were. you just got a little lost.
but you will never find yourself in someone
or something else.

beautiful being —
you were born as a soul with a body.
take off the person you have become.
take off all that is not soul.

you are moonfire and diamonds.
don't you know how much you shine?

april green

the parts you hide from yourself.
the ones you hear echoing through
your bones, like the dust of stars.

— these are the magic parts

paper wings

find it.

the thing
your soul aches for.
then.
let it consume
you.

april green

— when a dark cloud descends:

break into moonlight.
breathe night scented flowers.
listen to the world within you;
to the ocean in your veins.
swim in your own body.
hold your own hands.

(never forget what you're made from)

paper wings

you are the earth.
when a wave washes over
your heart.
listen.
your eldest mother
is warning you about
something.

— she is speaking to you all the time

you have
to erase
the beliefs
etched into
your bones.
the ones
others
wrote for you.
the ones
others
taught you.
the ones that
say
'can't.'
you have to
unlearn them.
you have to
plant
new seeds.
grow flowers
in all the places
you thought
you never could.

paper wings

that's the beautiful
thing about self love —
you wear it like a dress
and it becomes more and more
exquisite
with time.

find someone who will
share your falling tears.
who will hold them, until they melt
into the very essence of their being.

— without ever asking why

paper wings

— question

if they have stopped loving you,
could it be because you have stopped
loving yourself?

april green

if love is not returned to you
it is because you are giving it away
to everyone but yourself.

paper wings

and when i drown
in a warm and heavy sadness,
like a falling sunset; love —
it's you i surface to.

— it's always you

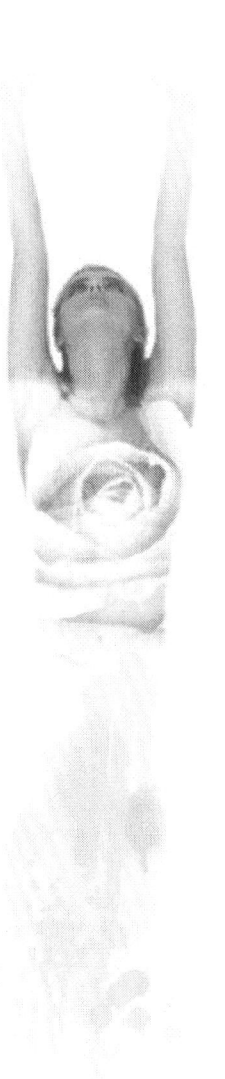

— the art of solitude

solitude is not loneliness.
solitude is one of the highest
forms of self–love you can reach.

please learn how to be comfortable
in solitude.
it will save you.
it will help you create something
with the hunger in your bones.

paper wings

— dark weather friends

be careful with the people who disappear
like stars in the daylight sky,
and only return
when the darkness is most upon you.

these are the ones who never want to see
your light.

april green

it will happen.
something will change.
something will carry you.

paper wings

there is an orchid
wrapped around my heart...tender
and strong and blooming.

a p r i l g r e e n

i am always bleeding new seeds.

— evolve

reclaim your growth.
you are still learning.
never forget this.
you will always be
still learning.

april green

– to my higher self

all these years of love
you have given me;
pressed inside my soul.
like a rare flower,
blooming from within.
all these storms
you have fought for me.
raging and burning and
freezing me out of my own skin.

how did i ever believe i was fighting
alone?

april green

— abandoned words

folded between
the flowers
in my throat.
swelling
and forming
and falling
from my mouth
like ancient prayer.

paper wings

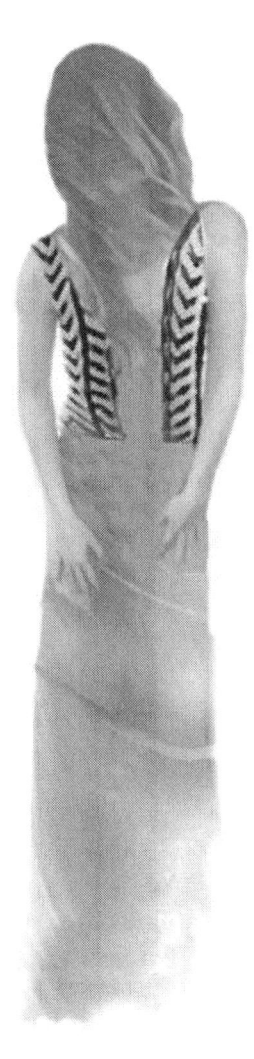

stay in your own skin...
it will always look
so beautiful on you.

april green

love april green

instagram & twitter: @loveaprilgreen

Made in the USA
Lexington, KY
22 November 2016